I0617557

Peace

A Spiritual

Way of Life

Christine A. Adams

Copyright

Hanley-Adams Publishing

Boxboro, MA 01719

www.hanleyadamspublishing.com

Foreword

When we are at peace with ourselves, we are more open to connecting with God, our spiritual source. Since we often live in a fast moving, technology driven, chaotic world, the search for peace becomes part of our spiritual journey. But how do we find peace?

As suggested in this series, we start by being grateful for what we have, and accept "what is" in our lives. We develop a true sense of humility and empathy towards others by recognizing that all people are created by God and have inherent worth and dignity. We forgive ourselves and others. We can confidently love ourselves, and others, as God loves us.

Then, as suggested in this book we make conscious contact with God through meditation, prayer, music, ceremony and rituals, or by spending time in nature.

Many people seek peace through acts of kindness, compassion, and service to others. These acts give purpose to our lives by connecting us to others and by bringing a peaceful "sense of wellbeing" to us.

Loving relationships, versus toxic relationships, foster peace. Learning to love yourself and God leads to self-acceptance which brings peace and inner confidence. Inner self confidence and faith help us with worry, fear and negative thoughts. We can slow down, be our own person and grow spiritually. We can avoid the stress of aloneness and separation.

In our search for serenity, the path might not always be smooth. Forces outside of us can cause turmoil and confusion. It's always "progress not perfection." No one maintains perfect peace at all times. If we do not experience discord we might not appreciate serenity.

Spiritual peace, or serenity, implies a quietude of the soul that comes in knowing yourself, and knowing God. It is the calmness that is always available to us because it is beyond the struggle, the human conflict of change. It is the spiritual gift that gives meaning to our humanity.

1.

Spiritual peace is a gift that you can cultivate and nurture over time. The search for serenity is the journey, not the destination. By practicing some of the suggestions outlined in this book, you can start to experience the benefits of spiritual peace is your life.

2.

Start your journey to serenity today by being grateful for what you have right now. Accept "what is" in your life. Practice humility by extending forgiveness to others and yourself. Love yourself and others as God loves you.

3.

Spiritual peace is the orchestration of our inner being. An orchestra conductor must carefully coordinate the efforts of the different musicians to create a harmonious sound. We must carefully coordinate our capacity and awareness for gratitude, acceptance, humility, love, forgiveness, and joy which creates a spiritual peace within ourselves.

4.

To attain serenity, it is important to maintain a harmonious, balanced lifestyle where our attitudes, values and behaviors are consistently peaceful. Seek out harmony, and balance and you will find peace! Seek out conflict and discord and you will find chaos.

5.

Peace and chaos are two diametrically opposed forces that are constantly at play in the world. Peace is a state of tranquility, order, and harmony. Chaos is a state of disorder, confusion, and violence. Life and reality happen somewhere in the middle, where peace and chaos are constantly in flux. We must seek out peace to remain peaceful!

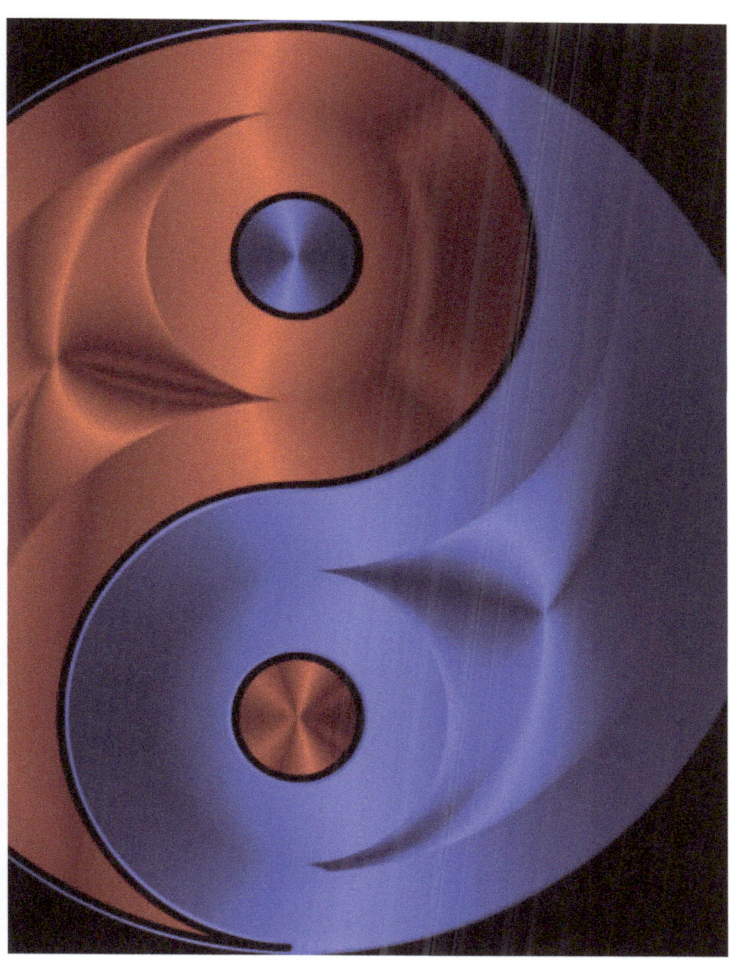

6.

Try to simplify! It is so easy to make very simple things in our lives overly complicated. Go back to the basics and always try to break each situation down into smaller "bite" size elements. Make a list, plan things out; but live "one day at a time".

7.

Spiritual peace gives us a powerful source of strength and resiliency. It's a feeling of calmness, which is often associated with a sense of wellbeing, even in the midst of stress, chaos, and crisis. When we achieve this resiliency, we are better able to withstand challenges and the setbacks ordinary life serves us. This calmness, and a lack of chaos or stress, can help us see the silver lining in all situations.

8.

Spiritual peace can be found through a variety of practices, like meditation, prayer, yoga, or spending time in nature. It can also be found through acts of kindness, compassion, or service to others.

9.

The search is different for everyone. Some need the peace of a formal religious service with reminders of God in music and prayer. Some find harmony and balance by the ocean, or the lakes and rivers. Some go to the mountaintops or gaze at the stars in the darkness of night.

10.

Create your own place of quiet reflection. In this place, you can turn off the world by "going within" to touch your soul! Find God!

11.

Listen to your favorite music. Let it wash over you and calm you. Let it bring up memories of past joys. Let it help you grieve. Find your quiet place, plug in your earphones and remove yourself from the noise of the world. Let your music help you through difficult situations that require patience and courage.

12.

Laugh as often as possible! Laughter is good for the soul. When you find someone who makes you laugh, cherish and nurture that friendship. It's a treasure worth protecting and preserving.

13.

Meditate regularly! Meditation can calm your mood and connect you to your inner self. It connects us to a power greater than ourselves, to God. Then, we aren't alone! Ever!

14.

God's works of nature can inspire us, humble us, and even have a calming, restorative effect on our mind and body. Find the beauty and power in nature and you will find the beauty and power within you.

15.

Change is an inevitable part of life, nothing stays static. The more effort we put into resisting change, the more uncomfortable we will become. When we feel change approaching, look for ways to embrace these opportunities. They are a great way to learn and try something new.

16.

When you're kind and have compassion for others, you will feel a sense of purpose and maintain your connection to others. When you're vengeful, unforgiving, and critical, you're living in conflict and disharmony with your inner self. That is the exact opposite of peace.

17.

In today's world of multimedia and technology, we are invited to relate to machines, not people. This dichotomy of "man vs. machine" can be frustrating, time consuming and unsettling. There are times you may have to say "No" to the machine to maintain a peaceful state.

18.

Your time is precious. If you're constantly choosing to relate to inanimate machines, you might find you're not refining your human relationships. God speaks to us through people, we are ONE in his likeness and we are all children of God.

19.

Love relationships can be beneficial to our wellbeing. They can help us slow down, make purposeful intimate connections, and avoid the stress of aloneness and separation. Good loving relationships can encourage us to be our own person, and grow spiritually.

20.

Toxic relationships can challenge us by creating conflict and stress. Dysfunctional situations and controlling partners inhibit spiritual growth. Remember a search for spiritual peace, harmony, and real love is a search for God. Avoid the detours of toxic relationships.

21.

When we are at peace with ourselves, we are more open to connecting to God, our spiritual source. Therefore, when we are at peace with ourselves, we attract loving people into our lives. Spiritual peace leads us on our journey to a more spiritual way of life.

22.

*The fact that you're reading this book about peace is your first step towards **more** peace. You're demonstrating an intention to have more balance and order in your life. "Humility" is simply having a realistic view of yourself and knowing you have limitations. When you're willing to learn and grow, you will find peace.*

23.

To love yourself is to know yourself! Inner self confidence comes from having a belief in your abilities and your overall worth. Then, you're less likely to be affected by negative thoughts and feelings. Without this mental negativity, you're less likely to compare yourself to others, or judge yourself harshly. Self-acceptance brings new peace!

24.

Inner self confidence helps you to be a good decision maker because you know what you can handle and what to avoid. It also helps you build strong relationships by communicating your true feelings. Good relationships and good decision making lead to a less stressful life which helps you to maintain a positive attitude. Thus, you have a greater sense of inner peace.

25.

Focus on your strengths and accomplishments. Make a list and review these accomplishments. Set realistic goals and achieve them. Celebrate each success! Surround yourself with positive people who support and believe in you. Don't berate yourself when you make a mistake.

26.

Be kind to your mind. What you say to yourself is important because you probably believe it at some level. What we believe about ourselves colors our entire existence. Our thoughts can cause internal stress. Listen to yourself! If you don't like what you hear, speak up and refute your unkind words. Love yourself!

27.

Spiritual peace leads to harmony, clarity, and completeness. Benefits of spiritual peace are less anxiety and stress, an increase in greater creativity, more restful sleep, and happiness and contentment.

28.

Spiritual peace requires a rigorous and honest understanding of the motivations behind our emotions and actions. It takes courage to search for the truth of our motives. Finding the real truth allows us to be open and find opportunities to improve.

29.

Forgive yourself and others for human mistakes. Understand that forgiveness has already taken place in the mind and heart of God. It is only a matter of time until we catch up, whether it is in this world or the next. Forgiveness of another brings peace. It is the gift you give, not to them, but to yourself.

30.

Think of the times you worried that some terrible things would happen and you were misled by worry and negativity. Nothing bad happened and miraculously your spirits were lifted and great events happened. You are not in control. Let go and let God!

31.

Find peace in the knowledge that God's will for you is joy. Other people, places and things do not have the ability to "make you unhappy, discontent or agitated." Happiness is an inside job, a choice you make each day. There is always something to be happy about even if it is only this very moment we share.

32.

Each day is alive with possibilities. Each moment is an extraordinary gift. You are right where you are supposed to be right now. This moment is all we have. Cherish it!

33.

Step out of the darkness of despair and worry. Find Hope in the light of God's Love, in the goodness of others, and the knowledge that you are a part of all creation, a child of God and there is nothing to fear!

34.

Matters of the spirit are learned in silence. Be still and know God. Matters of the world are generally resolved in the constant motion of change. Whether we are trying to achieve intrapersonal peace, societal peace, or even peace between man and the climate, there is usually a struggle. Progress is often made in noisy conflict but peace is experienced in quiet.

35.

Inner spiritual peace, or serenity, implies a quietude of the soul that comes from knowing yourself, and knowing God. It is the calmness that is always available to you because it is beyond the human struggle, and the conflict of change. Serenity is the "holy grail" of our human struggle, and ironically the gift that gives meaning to our humanity.

36.

The reason we included this book on peace in our Spiritual Way of Life Series, is because the pursuit of peace isn't only about creating a more peaceful world around us, but also about creating a more serene, spiritual world within ourselves. It is the key to happiness! This poignant quote by the Dali Lama sums up this important point: "Inner peace is the key to real happiness. If you don't have peace within, it is impossible to have real happiness in the external world."

— *Notes* —

— *Notes* —

— Notes —

Christine A. Adams

Christine A. Adams, M.A., has been writing about issues of addiction, relationships, spirituality, and education for over 32 years. She has over 2,000,000 separate books and pamphlets in print with works published in 44 countries translated into many languages. Christine, an English teacher, was also formerly trained as an addiction counselor in 1986. However, most of her writing parallels her life experiences. Her early writings were about the alcoholic marriage, adult children of alcoholics, teen alcoholism, and sexual addiction. Then came books about spirituality, relationships, grief therapy and education.

In addition, she has produced four very popular Elf Help children's books: <u>Happy To Be Me</u>, <u>Learning To Be A Good Friend, Worry, Worry, Go Away</u>, and <u>God Made Us One By One.</u> One of her best-known recovery books is the adult Elf Help gift book, <u>One Day At A Time Therapy</u> which is still selling in places like Taiwan, China, South Korea, Portugal, the Netherlands, Austria, Sweden, Indonesia, and Brazil.

Her other books include: <u>Gratitude: A Spiritual Way of Life</u>, <u>Acceptance: A Spiritual Way of Life</u>, <u>Spirituality: A Life Force</u>, <u>Seasons: Spiritual Meditations for Winter Spring, Summer, and Fall</u>, <u>Let Go, Let God</u>, <u>Teacher of God Holy Relationships,</u> and <u>ABC's of Grief: A Handbook For Survivors</u>. Other books include a fictional narrative, based on her years of teaching, called <u>The School Factory</u>, and romantic novel, <u>September Love</u>.

Visit her at www.christineaadams.com or

www.hanleyadamspublishing.com to find all her books.

Books by Christine A. Adams

Love: A Spiritual Way of Life

Acceptance: A Spiritual Way of Life

Gratitude: A Spiritual Way of Life

Seasons: Spiritual Meditations For

Winter, Spring, Summer, and Fall

Spirituality: A Life Force

ABC's of Grief – A Handbook for Survivors

Let Go and Let God

Teacher of God

Holy Relationships

Living in Love

September Love

Claiming Your Own Life

School Factory

Love, Infidelity, and Sexual Addiction

Gratitude Therapy

One Day At A Time

Learning To Be A Good Friend

Happy To Be Me

Worry, Worry, Go Away

God Made Us One By One

MD Hanley

MD Hanley has been a software engineer for over 30 years. He is passionate about technology and the way it constantly changes. He finds it to be a never-ending source of excitement and inspiration.

MD Hanley has always been an avid reader, and he developed a love of storytelling at a young age. His books include a financial thriller book called **Bit By Bit**, a cyberpunk thriller book called **Carbon Copy**, a science fiction book called **Quantum Mind**, and another book in the spiritual Way of Life Series of books called, **Humility: A Spiritual Way of Life**.

MD Hanley is an adventurer at heart. He enjoys hobbie like scuba diving, flying, and hang gliding. His experience flying through the congested New York controlled airspace hang gliding off a mountain top, or scuba diving on the Grea Barrier Reef have led to some interesting and unique insight into the world around him. MD Hanley is a talented softwar engineer, accomplished book designer, but also a gifte storyteller. He is passionate about technology, storytelling and adventure. His work is sure to entertain and inspir readers of all ages.

"Anyone can have a great story, but you need to be good storyteller to make it real and inspire imagination."

Books by MD Hanley

Bit By Bit

> Bit by Bit is a crime thriller about Gary McKeown, targeted for murder by his business partner after discovering his involvement in a bitcoin scam. Gary wakes up from a coma with no memory and embarks on a global chase to uncover the truth.

Carbon Copy

> Carbon Copy is a cyberpunk thriller about a world where every disease can be cured and aging is nonexistent, one man holds the key to unlimited power. In the wrong hands, it could mean the end of humanity as we know it.

Quantum Mind

> Quantum Mind is the second book in the **Quantum Genesis Series** is the story of twins, Kat and her twin brother Pat, who meet Alder who came to Earth over 5000 years ago. His ancient mission was to help planet Earth join a group of sentient planets quantumly connected around the universe. Does Alder complete his sacred mission?

Humility: A Spiritual Way of Life

> The fourth book in the **Spirituality as a Way of Life Series** describes how Humility: A Spiritual

<u>Way of Life</u> is a path of self-discovery. Humility helps to have a realistic sense of oneself, leading you to find the perfect balance of peace, confidence, and purpose in your life.

Also Available in the Spiritual

Way of Life Series

If you liked **Peace: A Spiritual Way of Life,** you can also find four additional titles in the **Spiritual Way of Life Series** currently in your favorite bookstore.

Gratitude: A Spiritual Way of Life

Acceptance: A Spiritual Way of Life

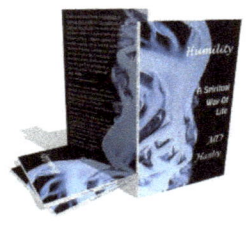

[Humility: A Spiritual Way of Life](#)

[Love: A Spiritual Way of Life](#)

Go to https://www.hanleyadamspublishing.com to link to your favorite bookstore.

Thank you for reading **Peace: A Spiritual Way of Life**! We hope you enjoyed it as much as we enjoyed writing it. If you did, we would be grateful if you could take a moment to leave a review on the site where you bought this book, or if you want o go to https://www.goodreads.com and share any thoughts or information you would care to leave about this book. Reviews are incredibly helpful for authors and also help other readers discover new books.

Thank you for your support and happy reading!

Christine A. Adams

MD Hanley